If Brambles Were Bookends

Collected Poems

Linda Bratcher Wlodyka

for my mom, Carol, who read poetry to me
and furnished her bookcases with poetry books so
that I might take interest and appreciate poems

Acknowledgements

Many thanks to all the publishers who included the following poems in their anthologies:

New Generation Beats 2023 Anthology, "In This Wild Existence"
The Long Islander, "It is Not Love but it Contains Loveliness"
First Literary Review East @www.rulrul.4mg.com, "Ethers Cobwebs"
Silkworm 13 Luck, "Crushing the Eyeliner"
Harbinger Asylum, "Origin"
Silkworm 10, "First Prize"
RE: Magpie Anthology Volume II, "First Prize"
Silkworm 15 Vision, "Whitewash"
Harbinger Asylum, "A Tale of the South Sea"
Goddess Anthology 2022, "What Mother Knows"
Goddess Anthology 2023, "Calling Card"
Silkworm 12 Survival, "Pattern"
RE: Magpie Anthology Volume II, "After the Dust Settles"
Silkworm 4, "Tidal Shift"
Journal of Modern Poetry 15, "Twilight's Not Eternal"
Harbinger Asylum, "Ode to the Beat Poets"
Remembering Jack Kerouac on his 100th Birthday, "It Was After I Read His Last Chapter…"

RE: *Magpie Anthology* Volume II, "Milkweed Meadow"
Silkworm 8, "My Poem is a Parachute"
Magpies: A Zoem Anthology, "Looney?"
Silkworm 14 Rise, "Drive"
my self-published Chapbooks:
Voices from the Blue Room, "Tidal Shift, What is Black?
Tick Tock, "Her-Rain-Bows," "Tainted Love," "Tick Tock,"
"The Swimmer," "Escapism," "Yellow Ink," "Secret Cottage,"
"My Ambrosia," "Tall Grasses and Willow," and "Goodnight!"
Silkworm 16: "Burst Wide Open"

"The heart, like the mind, has a memory. And in it are kept the most precious keepsakes."
-Henry Wadsworth Longfellow

Published by Human Error Publishing

www.humanerrorpublishing.com
paul@humanerrorpublishing.com

Copyright © 2023
by
Human Error Publishing & Linda Bratcher Wlodyka

All Rights Reserved

ISBN: 978-1-948521-06-2

The cover art for, *If Brambles Were Bookends*, was designed by the artist Rachel Esposito who brought Linda's vision to fruition with this phenomenal sketch art titled, *Lost Language*, referencing the last 2 lines in Linda's poem, "If Brambles Were Bookends." (Sketch ©2021)

Human Error Publishing asks that no part of this publication be reproduced or transmitted in any form or by any means electronic or mechanical, including photocopy, recording or information storage or retrieval system without permission in writing from Linda Bratcher Wlodyka and Human Error Publishing. The reasons for this are to help support the publisher and the artists.

Content

In This Wild Existence	12
It is Not Love but it Contains Loveliness	13
Ether's Cobwebs	14
Colorblind	15
Charmed by a Spirit	16
If Brambles Were Bookends	17
Uprooted Persimmon	18
flow	21
Burst Wide Open	22
Her-Rain-Bows	23
Crushing the Eyeliner	24
Origin	25
Scrutiny: Sara Steele Floral	26
First Prize	27
Tainted Love	29
No Forgetting	30
Falling	31
Heart Rhythm	32
Citrus Bomb	33
Touch	34
Whitewash	35
Tick Tock	36
The Swimmer	37
Her Idyllic View	38
A Tale of the South Sea	39
What Mother Knows	40
Potluck	42
If it isn't Real it Would be Nothing at All	44
It's What the Sign Says	45
Recompense	46
Calling Card	47
Pattern	48
After the Dust Settles	50
Credo	51
Placebo	52
Stone Cold	53

Escapism	54
Tidal Shift	55
Twilight's Not Eternal	56
Palette	57
Sieves	58
Like Mirrors in the House of Fun	59
What is Black?	60
Pilgrimage	61
Pale	62
Yellow Ink	63
Ode to the Beat Poets	65
Andy	67
Twiggy	68
It Was After I Read His Last Chapter…	69
Milkweed Meadow	70
Pink November	71
The Secret of Swirl	72
Secret Cottage	73
my poem is a parachute	74
lush	75
My Ambrosia	76
Early Ducks	77
Looney?	78
One Daffodil	79
MacDonald Brook	80
A Perfect View from the 38th Floor	81
Tall Grasses and Willow	82
Drive	84
Easy	85
Snow Effect	86
Goodnight!	87

In This Wild Existence

In this wild existence where we take claim
a life where wonder keeps us tidy inside our cocoons,
where dreamers shed tears then rebound,
where I proclaim more magic than mysticism.
Yet flowers bloom, children play, guardians loom,
lend safe haven, my own abilities evolve constantly.

Where your hand and mine cross miles
between mountains, valleys, longing for touch;
more desire than can breach a dam.
Where heart-blush looks good on paper valentines,
where the stick crosses a path, not a hindrance,
more than wind- swept.

My own two feet continue, I am in search of
the light, not at the end of a tunnel, instead
where solar rays find cracks, crevices, perforations-
seepage for their light. Where imperfections improve
like a quality controller gone manic.

Where flow not ebb sends forth currents, spirits thirst.
Where Luna's phantasm surrounds full pink moons,
exacting each poet's words- hieroglyphics, perpetual.
Where future inhabitants, peel off their facade,
mutter philosophies of sages; the poems we wrote.

It is Not Love but it Contains Loveliness-

An aura surrounds my state of being
like a margin without boundaries

it is pure intoxication. There is sunlight,
breezes, and the gentle sound of water.

It is not love, but it contains loveliness-
I feel its caress against my cheek.

It mesmerizes like an eternal flame,
it is a vibrating presence.

Its atmosphere is silvery blue. Instead of
clouds, I see feathers aloft.

Steady, like a continuum, I hear humming,
the pitch changes with the volume.

I see shapes evolve, then dissolve,
I am lifted into a rainbow's arc.

I feel wet drops on my hand,
it is comforting, I remain in my aura.

Neither stupefied nor amazed, I exist with
hopes I will never enter reality again.

Ether's Cobwebs

How intriguing your words appear. They
form nuanced phrases, intentional enticements.

A vortex spins your words into Ether's cobwebs.
I recognize that the words are yours when I drift nearby.

Ether knows to reinterpret your words into an intricate
language one of hope, song, sun, moon, twinkling starlight.

The strength of my soul echoes its response, a coherent
 transformation, an existential wonderment.

I readily accept Fantasy's invitation-time travel. I want to
discover causation, explain anomalies, share it with you.

One soul cannot endure this alone. Wrapped in silk,
enveloped together, we travel unknown stratospheres.

Colorblind

Drops condense on my etched goblet.
It's summer, you have moved even further away.
It's not relevant since my awareness is limited
by what I've misinterpreted. Instead, I am stimulated
by future events, the color of your poems.

Happenstance creates opportunities. A row of chairs
is full, save one empty chair next to you. When hesitation
leaves me speechless, I pivot to turn away, you tap the chair
say, "Sit here, it's not taken." I oblige.

Nearby, red wrought iron handrails connect to stage's banister.
A purple and pink polka dot doll is propped upon red truck.
She peers between each spindle cries out, "Mama," while
spinning tires struggle to climb up green ramp, I presume
a prop for another performance.

You turn to me, place your latest book in my hand.
Your cover art resembles Van Gogh's bedroom, instead
yours is neutral, black and white. You whisper that you
will be signing copies at the café nearby, tomorrow.

My first instinct is a congratulatory gesture, a handshake.
I smile place my hand on yours. You tell me what time
to meet you tomorrow. I nod.
I notice the café is titled, "The Colorful Mug."

I order an Irish Cream, adore the mug's green shamrock, its tartan
plaid. You hand me an autographed copy of your book. Pulling
colored pencils from my orange purse, Van Gogh's room
becomes a bright fortress. I hand you pencils. Every cover
evolves into an overture of brilliance, I read the word,
"colorblind" that you write boldly above Vincent's bedstead.

Charmed by a Spirit

Pass from one ghostly abode
to another, weight of pain
tortuous, unethical.

Random opponents forced out,
mired down as if suffocated
a foreign shelter.

A STOP sign shakes
like a flagrant flame,
more than fire in a kiln,

It rains ghosts instead,
count backward,
fierce winds howl.

A big bad boogey man
will break them, or
they will break him.

A brown leather key case
found, worn by years,
friction, cracked cowhide.

Key unlocks all pain
unresolved accusations
confirm an acquittal.

Sand is warm
residue more than ashes,
charmed by a spirit.

Fruit of the palm, salt
of the sea, pink roses
bloom endlessly.

They revel in a better version
of themselves, transcendence,
re-incarnation.

If Brambles Were Bookends

If brambles were bookends,
my hand would gingerly slide
three leather - bound volumes of
your original poetry books off
your shelf. Each word I read aloud
would place emphasis on your
interpretation, never mine.

This shelf, a mesmerism, shared
by bibliophiles, poets, sages,
wordsmiths, etymologists, and those
indulging in brambles, is a stoic shelf,
not meant to cast doubt. One
might inquire as to its architectural
stature, its organic origins, its ability
to protect itself. Like poison ivy it
innately lies in wait for its victim.

Each bramble nods as if to agree
that its purpose for being is more
than your poems, more than what
I meant to say, as if the beginning
never mattered, more substance
given to what lies in between.

And what lies in between feels
coarser than words spoken,
more trying than the discourse
between the end and the middle
of poetic words. The ones you
once made reference to as
pretentious; words brambled.

If brambles were bookends, I could
place a wreath adorned with blossoms,
not toxic fragrance like Rappaccini's
daughter exhaled, but fragrant like
honeysuckle, dew of nymphs. Each

blossom would enhance a bramble,
expose its prickly fibers,
tempt others to touch them.

If brambles were bookends, your
books, your words, would be
believed by every naysayer known.
No matter what scorn one feels, it
would be revealed in your words.
One could drink from the cup of your
poison nostalgia, interpret each phrase as
a critique to live by, secretly abhor the
temptation that your bramble belies.

I would return the three books.
I would place them spine side in,
revel in the fact that none of your
words were anything but bumbling
idolatry admittance of your innermost
phobias, deserving of a shelf of
scrub-brush bramble.

If brambles were bookends, I would
dismantle the barbs, allow them and
your books to fall away through the cracked,
rotted floorboards, to an eternal doom,
the lost language of you.

Uprooted Persimmon

More than the silence I ache for a whisper
wanting to know why all these turquoise bottles
were packed in a box too heavy to be moved
and why the linen napkins were now
posing as packing material when they belong
with fresh tablecloths and the shirt you wore
when I saw you last year.

More than the silence I ache for an envelope,
expressions of polite gratitude, a complimentary
high five to your recent successes, but there were
none to be had in a world so troubled by doubt, fear,
anxious people wanting something to reach for besides
another day of solitude preferable to the loud screeching
of tires that sped down the auto raceway three houses away.

More than the silence I ache for familiarity
the smell of clean laundry drying on the line
rose scents wafting across the meadow into a yard
so bright with orange lilies and yellow sun drops even
a caravan of carnival actors could not appear this brilliant.
Remembering a cascading waterfall coupled with our
drenching hair last summer, is all that I can fathom now.

More than the silence I ache for a small token,
a shiny bauble like a crow would place by your door,
a lost charm from a broken bracelet, the engraved message
now worn, weathered, beaten down by time,
hidden for years near a culvert where a young girl
climbed off a young boy after kissing him on the mouth
snagging her wrist amongst the grapevines where lovers hide.

More than the silence I ache for the taste of luscious fruit a
riper than ripe peach, strawberries, sugared rhubarb, fresh mint,
and the oolong leaves you placed in my ceramic pitcher, iced to
perfection like the cubes a bartender drops in a cocktail glass.
I recall a ten dollar bill that was left on the bar the last time I saw
you. You, always a generous patron. I was already out the door

walking to a place that I call home hoping you were in pursuit
behind me.

More than the silence, I ache for another page to turn,
I read your stories, a familiar poem you finished for me when
tears flowed down my cheek, landed against your forearm.
Even now you still blot the streaks of fluid that leave a salty
streak against our flesh, your tender kiss like a tincture. This
poem survives in all its first line repetition, like a cherished relic,
a coveted object. If it were not for the uprooted persimmon I'd
call out your name in tongues.

flow

rapid raging stream
exits over vertical drop
empties below into
riverbed displacing
rocks, roots, silt,
emergent rainbow
illustrious.

cavern's bedrock
securely affixed,
a rogue
blossom blooms,

like the daisy
pinioned
in her hair the
day she fell in
love.

Burst Wide Open

Not a piñata or the balloon from yesterday's party.
Not the bloom of a lily or a book opened for the first time.
Not fireworks or a tower of brass bells frantically ringing.
Not the crescendo of an orchestra or when a surprise party
erupts from nowhere. Not even a double rainbow.

More like when an infant babe exits a womb,
or when the sun blasts into full view riding along the highway,
even a wild hurricane's touchdown on land cannot compare to
the pulsing of blood through the veins, the flush, the weak in the
knees sensation, the heart- string- pull, the heart-song serenade.

Basking in the afterglow, euphoric burst wide open here and now,
this new-found love is not profound. It is more like your kin has
walked ten thousand miles to find you.

Her-Rain-Bows

Golden rays illuminate in
lost silence, rain showers drip.
Arcing across heaven
billowing white clouds
collide, a rainbow smiles.

Raindrops drench earth,
grasses emit perfumes
tropical and sweet.
Voluptuous lilies color
her world like rainbow beams.

A latent star peers
down to earth, arced
rainbow dispersed. She
only loves the rain when
the sun shines.

Illumination, one last ray.
Blooms drink in twilight,
passing rains. Upon her
flesh reveal permanent
arced rainbow stains.

Crushing the Eyeliner

REM refers to this chick as a sad tomato
not to be confused with a green tomato
or rotten tomato, just sad, wearing eyeliner.
 "Crush with Eyeliner" *

which gives credence to sad tomato
women that have those pretty
outlined eyes, yet I want to know,
what is this chick's dilemma?

Like it's this girl he has a crush on
walks three miles of bad road.
What's with being stuck on a bad road?
The dude is smitten and no matter how

she has invented herself, has he invented
himself as a tomato craver? Time to go
rescue her off that bad road. I'd like to
think this scenario ends with

red, ripe, tomatoes crushing all over
them like his love for her.
And the eyeliner?
It's intact like a charm.

*in reference to the band REM's
 song, "Crush With Eyeliner," from
their album titled, Monster

Origin

together they
        swim
                together they
                        crawl
                                together they
                                            walk.
they dance
        close together.

as if connected by a
tether,
        their togetherness
                in the wilderness
                        defies their
                                otherworldliness.

their harmonic oneness
                entirely monogamistic,
                      spiritual yet physical,
                            a survival of the fittest,
                                    defies the critics.
                                          even Darwin is optimistic.

Scrutiny : Sara Steele Floral

Coral lily blossom, not subtle,
A cracked-wide-open
display, wide and wild, like a seductress.
Her expose´ stigma, pollen.

On second look, head of Adonis,
blonde hair, chiseled jaw, he arches neck
forward, peering into golden tongue
lifeblood of birds, insects, butterflies.

He dreams of perpetual blossoms,
prostrate, he leans further into her petal cavity
held captive by gold dust, exotic fragrance,
Aphrodite's perfume infused.

First Prize

This month's all over
fifty shades of blue
makes life sad in
a peculiar way.
      Spent teacup,
      cream turned sour,
      his last brush stroke
      less pronounced than the ones before.

What is my nostalgia going to consist of?
      Story grids,
      jazz,
      my rock garden's newfound weeds,
      original poems.

I want proliferation of all that is right in the future.
For now modest growth is in order.
I want to reproduce all of it.
Would any joy become of
Puzzles - past, present, future?

Hypothetically speaking:
Take the blue prize ribbon winner to the county fair
show it off like he did those copper color clapboards
he stripped and painted,
shutters all maroon and regal.
He claims the shutters are sexy
      shuts out our view or lets others see in.

When downtown I ask a passer-by what kind
of food he liked to cook, he answered,
"Glazed duck." I smile while thinking about
mallards floating in the pond next door.
I reply, "Orange or raspberry glaze?"
It's the raspberry that he likes.

I pick wild raspberries each summer.
    Our e-mails exchanged
    for future culinary rendezvous.
    My bowl of berries overflows,
    others simmer into syrup.
    I'm entering this batch of jam
    in the county fair
    all maroon and regal,
    I bet I'll win.

Tainted Love

Beaten by raindrops
hurt beyond recognition
lightning crushed my tainted love.
Lost complacent fool,
I sit in silence
in the subzero wasteland.
Iced iris stiffens
all love becomes numb.

Arctic crust, glacial slide,
warm embracing melt.
Water flows as love takes hold.
A summer crush-
blossoms oozing
kissing bees sap nectar
drunk with elixir
tainted love stings.

No Forgetting

His tongue is his poetry. I remember when
he spoke there was no paper, no pen, no
forgetting. His announcement of autumn
described shadows how the sun shone, created
elongated angles different from summer.

His recollection of a first snow, how
snowflakes drift down to earth, how
he explained that the snow was a
blanket to cover earth's nakedness.
His long winded description of earth's

inhabitants how they stare, then retreat
to their structure, some have no shelter
always makes me self-aware of my own privilege.
His ever fanciful yet intriguing lesson influenced
the way I carried my emotion, the way I perceived

what I used to not openly admit.
My poetry benefited greatly from all that I
borrowed from those days of his reckoning-
the stage he built, his precipice, will be
embedded forever in the mind of the girl he loves.

Falling

The intervals between smile and breath
           where the intermittent pauses reveal your visage
and a metronome counts the times you said, "I love you,"
           while yearning persists, causes limbs to tremble,
heartbeat stagger, until both hearts palpitate in sync.

              There is no rational reason for it all.

All you wanted was to place your ear against my ribcage
     feel the pulse of blood rush through, place your hands
in my silken hair, along my jawline, caress the part of my lips
     where tongue reveals its sensuality, ask the burning question:

           Were we too much too soon?

Heart Rhythm

An emergent flow of motion, her stride sets her apart.
Poised, her lips curve, her smile intrigues him.

It is not just her, it's the breeze that she emits as she
walks, a floral scent of a botanical garden and how

her garment swishes. His mind is captivated by her presence.
She knows she's on his radar, her swagger titillates like

a mesmerizing aphrodisiac and he feels a desperate need
to stay nearby. Her presence becomes a subliminal flirtation.

The silence of the moment, this intensity of his feelings were
once hers, a reciprocation of adoration, physical beauty, passion,

one that changed the heart's rhythm, the air to exhale from their
lungs with a whimper, a sigh, evoking a spine tingling quiver.

Levitated by her presence his willingness to linger becomes an
unspoken invitation to her. She stands close beside him.

Riveted by his dark-eyed stare, she tiptoes close, whispers
in his ear, "it's okay you can take my hand." He places

it against his lips. He whispers to her, "It's like having
yourself in two different bodies." Their feeling of

acceptance into one another's world is cause for an
embrace. They appear as if Rodin sculpted these two

in their lip-locked pose yet he could never quite capture
the flush of their blood racing through their perfect

veins, as if one heart connected both bodies infusing a
synchronicity of erotic bliss held captive by their eternal kiss.

Citrus Bomb

Oranges, lemons, limes, a peach, squeezed.
The palm of my hand dripping, my tongue salivating.
Add seltzer, a scoop of cherry vanilla ice cream and pulse
at a low speed. Poured into a vessel, placed to one's lips,
tongue and mouth welcome citrus tingle, it's inevitable
lusciousness. It drips down the chin in rivulets to the décolleté
until it seeps between the breasts sticking to cleavage.
A soft soaked cloth with body soap is placed into
the palm gently caressing the skin, rinses and lifts
the residual juices. Without you here to imbibe,
I touch towel to skin, imagine the delicacy of
your tongue cleansing me.

Touch

Fluid lips blush, a blot of chardonnay
caresses them. He stares across the
table, eyes affixed on her lips.

Lips pouty, velvety rose petals.
Her tongue, lips, speak to him
curvature of lips dizzy him.

Wine goblet presses between her lips
pours through to tongue. She swallows,
savors the chardonnay. He savors her.

Her fruited breath passes through her lips
like an aromatic breeze sent streaming. He
inhales it deeply, longing for her lips to meet his.

Goblet waits for lips, lips to quaff the wine.
His desire lies latent, he licks his lips while
he waits for the lips of a cherub, a goddess.

Her ruby rosebud lips rare dewy from wine.
Lost in reverie he closes his eyes. Without
warning or advances her lips incoherently touch his.

Whitewash

Color splotches drip, streak, dab.
I watch your brush create.
Your horizon where water and sky meet
are more than a sunset, an embodiment
of peace waiting for the night sky.

I see strokes form. A couple standing
on a stone bridge embracing like they
melted together there for eternity.

An old farmhouse sits amidst pasture and creek,
its crumbling chimney wracked by the wind.
One lit window glows peachy orange.

Always your images progress, like your painting
titled, "Husband of Bryn Mawr," how this character's
white windblown hair and flexed bicep reveal his
years of labor, melancholy expression, lips slightly
apart, teeth clenched. His hazel eyes affixed on his pasture.

Your seaside landscapes are more than a brush stroke's
caress. I feel the tide's ebb and flow, granular sand in
between my toes as paint touches canvas, moves the color
like a swirling spoon relocates cream in a cup of joe.

I imagine the Husband of Bryn Mawr displaced, sitting
in the farmhouse waving to me from the lit window. As the
light dims his hand disappears, all fades to gray. The last
glimpses of a setting sun, your stroke of whitewash blinds me if
only for seconds. I turn to find you are gone, I hang your
paintings on my wall.

Tick Tock

twisted twilight
tainted with thorns
pierces my skin
blood pools
then drips,
I've wondered where you've been.
mysterious man
all whiskers
and words,
I hear your
indecipherable moan
rise above a gravestone.
bend ear to earth
lush turf.
night crawlers
squirm. haven
for crows,
dandelions and worms.
father time, tick tock.
whiskers, blood, thorns,
petals disclose
shadowy rose
left to repose
a single tear flows.

The Swimmer

The woman stands alone six feet from shore.
Her feet suffer the remnants of August's hurricanes
which teach the ocean to rise and crash forcibly
showing no mercy to the swimmer's need to exit.
Sea-spray, a rapid firing surf and undertow

ripping anything in its path forward then back.
Her staggering, swaying, will not cease.
Love the tide as she may, no comfort here today.
Desperately she inches uphill toward shoreline.
Piled gray rocks, seaweed, a line of demarcation

where undertow and tide meet. Spinning rocks turbine
forces mimicking raging waterfall, she totters onward.
Hopeless, she peers out over ocean waves the ones
she has swam in for all her years, sacred water-
god purifying. "Will she make it to shore?"

is her endless query. Lost to the sea, she accepts her plight.
Lover of marine life, nautical instruments and ships
if her fate lies with the sea she must accept this-
her dirge. Once a landlubber now possessed by
unmerciful tides, creeping and crouching landward

her groan is deafened by the sea's. Her
mind swirls in eddies recalling loved shipman
of old; Captain Ahab, Seafarer and the Ancient Mariner.
No sympathy from the wild sea, these captains sail on.
Likewise the swimmer's fate unknown, no albatross to

guide her home. Upon viewing tidal surge, gaining her
foothold, a fair-haired woman emerges, angel of rocky shoals.
Inches separate them, wings stretching upward
hands connect, the saving grace of ocean's wrath,
the angel gently sets the swimmer beside the raging sea.

Her Idyllic View

He caresses a sea sponge, brushes her cheek,
flexes his bicep like a dolphin in search of his mate.
Immersing into the aqua water slippery plankton
flows, underwater path leading to a reef, *Reef of
Mermaid* as it is told in legends, pirate's lore.

Sand bars piled high from tidal wash, high tide
coerces coast guard vessel adrift, foaming surf,
whales, seals, chased by hungry great white
sharks, threatens swimmers forced to wade in the
shallows, fog rolls in, lighthouse eyes shore.

He caresses the urn he carries, protects former
life in the crook of his arm, while seeking the view
she loved, river meets sea, brackish holy liquid carries
memories, her idyllic view. He is here alone, scatters
her remains like an inverted powder puff toppled.

Her anatomy torched, her head, luxuriant hair, limbs,
torso, groin, of his true love. Oh her heart, his heart, her brain
so fascinating that she chose him, now flows downstream
into swirling eddies, reminding him of her twirling her hair
around her index finger, now flows out to sea, out to sea.

A Tale of the South Sea

"Let me look into a human eye; it is better than to gaze into sea or sky; better to gaze upon God."
                         Herman Melville, *Moby Dick*.

After the black nights
and red days faded
he thought better,
kept refuge here.
Shipwrecked, he's
washed ashore,
somewhere in the
South Sea.

He prays as if the eye of
every storm held God in its pupil.
He stares at the coastline,
squints at the apparition,
a naked woman, beautiful,
alone, yet with child.
He approaches slowly,
she neither moves nor speaks,
she does not breathe.

"It is better to gaze upon God," he thinks.
Falling to his knees he prays for another sunset,
another sunrise, another fearless day of hope.

What Mother Knows

For my mother, Carol

My mother once said she would fill my bucket.
Mother said the bucket should be filled with hope.
I asked, "How? How does one place hope into a vessel?"
Mother aptly described her experience of filling;
"Hope" she says, "is an ingredient derived from trust and faith."

I then ask as to how one can acquire enough trust.
Mother replies, "In believing in yourself, your intuition,
knowledge, gratitude. The respect you give returns to you
ten-fold." "Really?" I reply. Mother continues,
"You need faith to compliment trust to have a bucket of hope."

I stare at mother wondering if I ever will believe
enough in faith to realize that trust will give me hope.
Mother then says, "No need for you to fret.
Faith is what you have inside your spirit,
the part that feels like all is well, the simple
nuance that gives life meaning, lets your inner soul rest."

"Wow! Okay," I say. "I must already harbor
faith since what you describe, is a genuine feeling
in my soul." Mother then asks "When will you fill
your bucket with hope?" "Gee", I reply, "The two
ingredients we speak of trust and faith, are readily
available within me, but how am I supposed to empty
myself of these in order to fill the bucket?"

Mother chuckles and peers off across the late
afternoon horizon. The sunset gleams golden,
enveloping the silver clouds. The indigo sky fades
to dusty pink as the sun begins to slip lower.
The full moon etches and expands into the evening sky.
The two entities, sun and moon, collaborate, if for
only a brief while. Clouds part and drift revealing
the black night sky. The brilliant gems of the universe
sparkle, leaving me riveted.

"See the big dipper spread across the sky?"
my Mother asks me. "Yes the dipper," I respond.
Mother continues, "The dipper is to gaze at,
to meditate upon, for you to take in the spectacular light show."
"Look," I shout to my mother, "There's my bucket,
the little dipper, twinkling. And over there a falling star
has drifted into its open vessel. "That's hope filling up
your bucket." mother replies. "Really Mother?" I say,
how can I acquire enough hope, unless the stars know
trust and faith abide within me?"

Mother exclaims, "I knew all along that your bucket
would fill to the brim with hope. Now look up at
the sky again. More stars are raining down into
your little dipper. Now you have more than enough.
See, hope overflows." Mother smiles then advises,
"Now go spread hope throughout the world."
I respond hesitantly, "In the morning after I've
had a good night's sleep."

And so from that day forward, as the moon shines
and the stars create their illustrious showers,
hope replenishes itself continuously.
I did not talk to mother again for many moons.
She fell away like a brilliant star, spreading bright light.
I never knew until several years later, when
mother appeared, that Hope was mother's given name.

Potluck

I

That's what it was,
potluck.
Me, brunt of their joke.
Nobody shows up.
Just me and a dozen deviled eggs
sliced in half to feed twenty four.

II

I am eating the eggs,
the decadent eggs.
I cannot eat them all.
I'll leave them here for somebody else.
I bet nobody will touch them.
Did I mix up the date?
I'll have egg on my face.

III

I hear a car pulling in
to the Lichenstein lot.
It's the egg lady with her tote bag.
She comes to the door.
I ask her, "Are you here for Potluck?"
She says, "Do you want to buy eggs?"

IV

I want to leave but the egg lady
gives me a home-baked cherry pie.
She did not want me to feel stood up.
She says, "It's not fun to feel like a nobody."
She makes me feel like somebody.
Before she arrived I felt pot-out-of-luck.

V

I thank the egg lady for coming.
I offer her some deviled eggs.
She says, "Yuck," then apologizes.
I understand that she might not want
to eat eggs all the time.
We sit and eat cherry pie together.

VI

The egg lady has to leave now.
I want to leave too,
to stay here longer alone, makes
me feel like a nobody again.
She reminds me I am a somebody.
She appreciates that I like her pie.
I appreciate that I can buy free-range
eggs from her any time.

VII

"Who says you need
 more than two foods and two
 people at a Potluck?"
As I step out the door somebody
yells out, "Who's in there?"
I answer, "Nobody."

If It Isn't Real It Would Be Nothing At All

It is desire more than adoration stealing my
attention even practicing will not improve the chances.
It swarms with self-doubt yet blossoms like hope.
It manipulates my brain as if hanging on every word.
Scholars, muses, poets authenticate every line,
the words talk to me from the page like
reassurances gone awry. I hear the voice read,
I memorize its flavor. No aromatics, no citrus,
no healing balm or cleansing sage can lend its
purity to the sanctity I embrace. It thrives on
time and its passing. To vanish is to perish.
This inspiration is a continuum. Reality is not
an anomaly. It is a subtle belief, more than
human hearts dare hang their life on.

It's What the Sign Says

                ekphrastic from Sydney Gauthier's artform,
                                   Hierarchy

The sign's message one duplicated word
super imposed upon itself like dead matter,
makes it clear the black ink leaves smatter,
the artwork evokes untold chatter,
an ability to stay politically correct
is that what really matters?

Why did it lead to a throng who scatters?
Don't allow an obscene blather,
don't leave a body in a tatter.
This message was not meant
 to go rogue or shatter,
the sign repeats, gets exponentially fatter.

A message to enhance the ages
offer advice like sages,
located on a map, no more cages
no blame or digressions,
no reason for enrages.
Let the sign sing with a multitude of voices.

It's a civil liberty deserving of all people's rejoices.
It's because Gauthier's art form, *Hierarchy*, was created.
It moved me like the poetry of Amanda Gorman.
The word matter just a prompt to try and explore it.
Here I write and expound on ideas, notions, all I'm
really trying to emphasize is dignity, devotion.

Recompense

Collapsing into the valley
the last ray of sunlight
illuminates, sparkles off
quartz staircase, the one
which beckons her to the
ancient crypt where she
descends for her mourning ritual.

Like a trial, an interrogation,
she feels wound up inside,
like a spring-loaded weapon
waiting to explode.

To eradicate hostile emotions,
to relinquish angst,
to feel justice for the wrong
inflicted on her people,
to set her spirit free she

kneels by the crypt inscribed
with family members names.
Wailing, she prays for the dead,
their oppression she never witnessed.
She reads the chronicles, imagines
the treachery her ancestors endured.

Dusk falls. Pained by her own
vulnerability, she wipes away tears,
gazes back at quartz staircase that
ascends onto the grassy plain,
then wanders back to the City of Love.

Calling Card

William Wordsworth said, "The World is too Much With Us."
Am I too much for this world?

Where integrity is written off as a misnomer,
empathy a weakness, judicious thought, a dream.

I hide from the window's light as it passes through clear glass
panes, allows my fleeting fancies to reflect, refract, refrain.

Pure and unadulterated respect, will it be tolerated?
Is there compromise in the name of kindness?

These shoes we walk in, do they share a stranger's feet?
A mile is not enough, a lifetime too long.

Sensibility- Is it treasured?
Liability - is it cautionary?

As we hang in the balance,
Shouldn't trust + authenticity=comfort?

Blood flows like a rushing river through my veins
during melt season. Am I here for a mission?

Yes. If you listen closely you can hear a subtle drip,
like melting ice, like seeping red wine, like an

enigmatic lilting voice. If the world and I are way
too much, may this be my calling card; scepter,

olive branch, an ancient, exotic gilded trinket, excavated
deep from a humble Egyptian goddesses' tomb.

Pattern

After she unfastens a hook
Lays the rope in a pile with slack
Turns toward the blaring sun
Wind gusty against her back
Dogs bellow then resound
Air seeps from bicycle tire
Flower vase reveals dead stems
A feeling that being late can inspire

A tire lies completely flat
She turns toward the setting sun's beams
Empties water from vase, discards stems
Dogs sleep, dream buried-bone dreams
Slack rope needs putting away
A hook she unfastened on stair
No wind to cool her bed
Stay up late, spinning fan by her chair

It's no use, she cannot ride to town
Bicycle disabled, damaged tire
Dogs whimper cannot get to sleep
Slack rope tangles, no hook to desire
Gale wind has smashed flower vase
Behind clouds sun cannot reveal light
Alarm clock does not keep time
Late shadows have haunted her night.

Upon awakening her bicycle's repaired
Enables her to do errands in town
Dogs sit on the porch no despair
Slack leash is unfastened for now
Dried flowers alongside a vase
Puffy clouds sail along in the breeze
A clock chimes announces the hour
Moon rises casts shadow on trees

Her life a pattern of things
Events mundane, fill her days
Bicycle not missed, a car in garage
Dogs die, then are replaced
Sky's cloud pattern like a refrain
Wind blusters blows curtains askew
Vased flowers stand test of time
It's tragic that nobody knew

After the Dust Settles

It was the hub-bub & all the honey-do
lists & life passing us by.

It was the elders seemingly aging faster,
babies growing at warp speed.

All the while holidays, gifts, toys piling,
event-surety, coming of age.

Joy, joyous, joyously, ever-yearning,
deep breaths hum-squelch.

Living then not living, missing
like a ghost-walk, spirit guide.

Memories remembered beyond recall,
hole in the heart remembering.

Make whole the un-whole, cool off,
cultivate rare snow, jewel-frost.

Coursing through the ages,
no obliteration, strife-mania.

No boomerang effect, brick wall effect,
voice-overs a way with no exit.

Suggest yellow eye a-sleep,
suggest red mouth mute-seep.

Like leaves feathery, wispy,
like winged nymphs in flight.

Polish gem beyond reckoning,
whiter than white-wash.

Indulge beyond translucent moon,
caress fire-light, transient flume.

Credo

Stillness, dark and obtuse,
this is how it is before the eclipse.
Seldom can one remember
a transcendence so serene.

When I watch the school
of fish gather in the shallows,
spawning their offspring,
currents camouflage the brood.

Thought rules universe
emerges as theory:
religion, philosophy, science,
makes no matter to the minions.

Their credo will bear witness to
whatever transcendence transpires;
whether white, black, red, gray, translucent,
what is now becomes undone.

Placebo

Inside all this want, a cure.
Remain silent, feel ill-disposed
admit risk, then flourish.
The fact of the matter is

what you swallow ends up as
the end result; warranted or not,
the placebo inside you yearns
to be authenticated like a void filled.

Stone Cold

*Ekphrastic after Edward Hopper's
"Automat" 1927*

It's as if he knows,
knows loneliness is pervasive.
That gal with her cup
left to sip on coffee.

He paints. Brush punctuates,
crosses t's and dots i's
of life with distraught gloom,
as if no one ever knew her.

Stark yet stoic, frozen in time
and space, her fashionable
hat adorns her, like a storefront
mannequin - stone cold.

Escapism

Mosaic dream haunts me still
until the dawn
I lie awake
revelations come
glimmers of that horrific era
will not elude this
comatose trance

Oh protector- daylight
grant that this mosaic dream
be washed and tumbled
through crashing sea foam
churning its almighty force
against the jagged cliffs of time
release this sorrow, purify my soul

Mosaic dream returns now at dusk-
the pillow talks incessantly
mimes motion displaying fragments
my life, askew-
the ivory tower,
rose-colored glass,
are smoke and mirrors after all,
time, jig-sawed, refuse

Oh rest, relief I crave
may tomorrow's torment lessen,
no gray, no haunting shadows
release the karmic light
Indigo prisms spinning-
I swallow elixir of awareness
perpetual mosaic dream
pre-deceases me

Tidal Shift

Salty surf surges toward the shore,
shores far away from friends, family,
one that castaways cling to, a harbor,
humbles them while yearning for safety.

The shore wanderers shipwrecked
bring their dirty disease, dirty dealings
onto this Isle of Idiots surrounded by
something eerie, teeth, incessant
clicking wily, wicked inhabitants.
Nowhere comfort for vagabonds.

Natives ward off wanderers tantalize
terrified intruders. Blood-letting, hexes,
voodoo, warning stay your distance.
Tremendous turning tide roaring its
rueful yarns nocturnal noxious doom
lurking lair of natives, watching, listening.

Wanderers unwelcome, weary, horrified,
helpless, hindered. Natives beat drums,
incantation. Forecasting derelicts demise,
castaways succumb, carnage.
Strewn carcasses cover coastline.
All's well on the Isle of Idiots.

Twilight's Not Eternal

light diminishes.
stolen by night,
shadow catcher scalps
the last sun rays.
pointed rock mountain
casts its last craggy shadow
reflection on the red clay trail.

fire scorches rock.
clay melts, molds,
adheres to the promise
of another sunset,
another sunrise,
another burnt offering,
pungent ash, cold.

Palette

It was the gray furniture I chose to buy.
The pandemic caused shortages.
I wasn't sure the likes of elephant skin gray, dolphin gray,

or tree bark gray could wow or enhance my living room.
I say, "It's the yellow walls that matter." Benjamin Moore
paint offers a Hawthorne yellow which glows amber.
It is also an exterior color seen on two hundred year old
colonial houses. It suits my walls.

I chose poetic pillows: "Happiness depends upon ourselves."
Not that I love throw pillows all that much. They cannot replace
a bed pillow for comfort. Decorators call them accent pillows.
Leave them on an unoccupied chair, accent complete.

A crafter from Etsy made them. I presume they saw this room.
The pillow is gray, yellow, white and black, patterned in
swatches, a random collage. Butterflies, three black chickens,
(which I could have sworn were crows from the online image),
vines, leaves, flowers and a hashtag of stripes comprise this
collage. My curiosity kills me when it comes to the chicken wire
fence. It looks like the chickens flew the coop proudly perched
up on that branch.

I add some furniture scarves which are the same color as the
pillows. Tiny flowers, berries, vines, kittens, butterflies and tiny
black, white-haired nymphs which appear to present as female
sit amongst the flora. I believe I chose this wonderland to keep
fantasy alive in my living room, lend some magic to a mundane
moment.

New lamps seem to be in order. They are metal, donning black
leafy vines, with white shades. I imagine the cats and nymphs
will someday escape their lair, hoist themselves onto the vined
lamp, sit pretty grinning at me like the Cheshire Cat. Then they'll
swing off the lamp, plop into my cold drink, talk gibberish while
swimming in my Pinot Grigio.

Sieves
2020

Planks banked against slippery slope of unrenumerated
time without a sense of being. Falsehoods muttered,
spewing hypes, tropes, cramping your untamed
mind into a boggle of strewn mutants, lackluster, until
an oncoming dystopia takes hold.

How much of this fine-tuned mockery will endure?
Countless lessons, leanings, learnings, loosely-tied
amidst this mange. A quintessential dogma erupts from
mouths. One simple request posed to doctors, a cure;
medical science should not nuance or hyperbolize.

Relinquish each involuntary spasm, pulse, pivot
toward eruptive euphemisms. Sequester boasts
downstream - empty into the River Styx, then segue
upstream a cold spring of purity, flush, flow, filtered
currents bordered by phlox, filigreed Queen Anne's lace.

Quantify, qualify, question. Subliminal messages
matter. The hard fought heart encased in its
shrine will never preach debauchery, likewise it
undresses untruths, nakedness equals proof.
Fools on parade wear mask-like sieves.

Like Mirrors in the House of Fun
2020

It was not the rim's edge,
or sylvan, silver trail,
or icicles dripping a rivulet.
nor was it the slush enveloping.

It was more like snowdrifts billowing
in concentric patterns, like an embellishment.
Claw of crow, paw of hare, wing of hawk,
imprint their images like a template.

The shimmer of daystar,
crystalizing, cold thaw,
earth a prism like mirrors in the house
of fun it reflects, refracts, illuminates.

Naked unearthing.
Moistness breathy,
wets 'n washes.
All that is sordid touches down.

On the rim's edge,
slush envelopes like hushed
wings embracing Gaia. Warm
breezes calm, coax, while the
globe spins, pivots, races, in its
mortification. Hail the scientists
who once again find the cure, hail
earth's people for staying the distance.

What is Black

muted shades-silver-gray-grayer-grayest-then black-midnight black-no moonbeam-charcoal strokes-hand nimble-steady sliding-stroking-rubbing to & fro-slowly-rapidly-depicting darkness- dismal air-rain clouds-ozone-particles-industry-coal-silver-gray-grayer-grayest-then black-sooty black-no moonbeam can penetrate this miasma-living lungs disintegrated-toxins-igneous matter-silver-gray-grayest-black-the formidable sun ablaze-searing-orange-red-conflagration-ruinous to nimble hands-no charcoal-no strokes-no rubbing-no sliding to & fro-
no moonbeam-blacker than black-eternal black-a black hole-
an abyss-no other color-nothing remains-the meltdown is complete.

Pilgrimage

Insular it is.
Beings deeply entrenched
find this habitat alternative,
strained, estranged.

It is like that;
on an island, a desert, a mountaintop.
Colonies exist unto themselves
until upheaval denigrates.

An apocalypse
rends them homeless,
blasts them skyward,
lands them defenseless.

A hapless embodiment of
wayward pilgrims float into
frigid currents. Flotsam flourishes.
Sea dwellers multiply.

Metamorphosis ensues.
Gives birth to an atrocity:
dark, deranged, derelict,
it mutters incantations.

Ocean's tide lackluster,
sings a treachery.
Souls repent, slither,
beyond where whirlpools suck.

The lucky ones inhabit a lost
city, others presumed missing,
spun into a time warp.
Is this the new beginning?

Pale

Pale is not her preference.
Purposely quoted, her proposal
is not a perfect request
nor is it possible to fulfill.

She chooses beige, a muted tone
offsetting other purposeful choices.
Purple looks like what one professor
expected, albeit repugnant.

Again she ponders practical applications
that contrast not perpendicular to her original.
Are there possibilities to explore?
This calls for preponderance.

She pours over minions of choices
knowing it's painstakingly worthwhile.
Convinced of her inability to pass as
professional, she remembers colors

not desirable; moldering feathers
pinioned behind pastel birds, persnickety
posers roosting high up in palm trees in
places like Panama, Pebble Beach and Penapolis.

Half-heartedly she presumes pale will be
passed on as eggshell, ivory, bone, alabaster.
Yes, alabaster will get her to fulfillment which
is reminiscent of infancy, her primordial pale.

Yellow Ink

Liquid flows from pen
drips golden
I knew the day
would glisten
that God would listen

Sweat drips from
her brow at noon
handkerchief blots,
up in the clouds
a balloon she spots

He dries teardrops
from her young eyes
she mounts her pony
watches sun rise

Yellow sunbeam
brighten horizon
big sky opens vivid blue
clouds cast pearlescent hue

Wispy tendrils
crown forehead
curly lashes frame
eyes of green
her golden tresses gleam

Baby sleeps
so it seems
suckles thumb, sighs
rolls over, sweet dreams

Aged couple rock,
sing, speak
the porch boards
recant with every creak

Puppy whimpers, kitten
purrs, sun slips down
behind God's earth
moon's aglow, within a mist
candle drips like yellow ink

"Ode to the Beat Poets"

it's not the transient soul
it's the transient sole

it's not the tire that screeches then implodes
it's not the stench of flesh baking in
the sun but the candy sticky crunch
it's not a carafe of wine that leaves a
grape stain or that the
Madonna's tongue is lily white
it's not how purity sings but how grace
flows flows takes ahold hold & endures
      it's not anybody (you know) that
      leans over a 40th story
      balcony in midtown Manhattan

or how a red line stains the pavement
it's not what you like or want or anything
you can control it's what hangs down from
park trees & flag poles & what flaps from a
car's antenna that
      sparks a light incandescent- blind,
      brighter than the brightest sun.

it's everything far & near
    here or there that whispers the law
of the land that fences you in or fences you out
    that taps you on the shoulder
& pushes you into the confines of four walls
    with murals-ugly yet exotic,
      with fading streak tugging at
        your soul soul.

it's accelerating to 100 mph on a
       straight stretch of highway
       after exiting the foothills of the
Rocky Mountains travelling with the convertible top down
          in a black 1958 T-Bird racing onward through
       sand cacti tumbleweed Las Vegas then into
Northern California where San Francisco Bay's
       fog stares you down
wipes the mud from the soles of your dirty feet
          then shines.

Andy

Andy Andy, show me your groove.
Andy Andy it's Pop Art you paint so indelibly cool.

Campbell's tomato soup & Coco-Cola
was your iconic claim to fame, your paint splashes electrified
Marilyn, Elizabeth, Mick Jagger, John Wayne & that color burst
for Mao Zedong how could it be wrong?

Andy Andy, "The Factory" made your legend grow,
Andy Andy Studio 54 was all gaga over you.
Andy Andy, you survived that miserable bullet Valerie shot at you.
Andy, Andy, some think you exploited commercialism cause that
        looked good for you.

I like to think you criticized materialism and celebrity as the
1960's embraced you. You're like a rainbow, so much hue.

Andy, Andy I wished you painted anything for me
        even one splash of love will do.

Twiggy

Oh Leslie Hornby we love your name,
aka Twiggy gives you attention & fame, fame.
I buy a 3-ring binder emboldened with your visage
I stare at it every day, day.

Those twigs you draw above your cheekbone
& below your eyes, an iconic look that makes up your face, face.
Three layers of false eyelashes painted seems tame, tame.

Your Brit tongue and boyish hair drives us wild, wild.
You are the envy of every girl child, child.
Some say androgynous yet I tend to disagree,
your slight figure becomes the rage, rage.
Your fame leaves you saner than sane, sane.

So much for modeling you also act and sing.
Your songs are of luv, luv, your album,
"Romantically Yours" is my plug, plug.

It Was After I Read His Last Chapter…

I felt a snippet mind blown.
It caught me in a mystic foothold.
Like my existence was a fractal lifespan.
My thoughts became a mosaic mind-bend.

I looked at the horizon-
A splintered rainbow.
Like Alice, I wanted a slide down a rabbit hole.
Instead, I traversed a centrifugal wormhole.

A pendulum tranquilized, a monocle
blindsided, due to a pill capsulized,
because of a third eye downcast. It was
evident no welcome mat can make a mad dash.

I thought about the derelict blowhole.
A whalebone emaciated, encrypted
below a tombstone, lying aside a martyred
hourglass, accentuated like a purple sand blast.

A peel - here decal extricated, worse still
a beating heart infatuated, a roving
spirit supplicated. The caw of crows
intoxicated, a peal of bells reciprocated.

The lack of water instigated.
A divining rod's purpose evaluated.
A douser exclaims, "underground wells
not renovated," a virgin rock fracture anticipated.

This perpetual poem may be abbreviated,
or laid down as dust, exterminated, or live
on as a mantra then redacted.
I prefer it be a comic truce, extenuated.

Milkweed Meadow

Frosty dewdrops cling-create miniature rainbow
upon milkweed pod. Dew thaws under December's
warm sun. Lithe faeries bathe, dip each toe, finger,
fragile wingtip with deft intricacy into blessed liquid.

Each dewdrop collapses, implodes, surrounds faeries
now ensconced inside their glittering dome.
Cleansing ritual, intense flutter.
Wingspans burst effervescent bubble.

Infant faeries emerge as if the heat of this
December's sun incubates new faerie generation.
Elder faeries lie prostrate quietly chanting,
inviting the whole universe to celebrate.

When the freeze of winter returns,
elder faeries commit to activities,
their young now grown in search of
milkweed pods, frozen dewdrops.

Sun's rays give rise to the thaw. Once bathed,
faeries perform flutter dance, anticipate
dewdrop burst. A proliferation of life swarms in
milkweed meadow. Elders ecstatic celebrate their coming.

Pink November

Sumac display- entering Lake Mansfield Road,
Great Barrington, MA

Leaves still cling to trees.
Sumac leaves fade to pink,
a sheen, silvery glow.

Silvery pink leaves are strewn like an open-weave
lace, like necklaces strung delicately with care
as if decorated for celebrating the coming of love.

Like a ribbon strewn along a path to find one's
way out, silvery pink appears before passersby without
warning. No admission fee, splendor, a feast for eyes.

My eyes ask the trees how it came to be:
choice of color, the intermittent arrangement,
a pink so delicate even silver came to adorn it.

I imagine a master painter drizzling pale pink paint,
like a faceted jewel, a silver hue, a phantasmal beacon,
artistry beyond reason stands the test of November's time.

Like fairies in motion pink leaves drift away.
Pink November's pageantry now bed for decay.
Pink November, fades to the grayest of grays.

Secret of Swirl

The ending circled back to the middle.
No one can read an absent beginning.
The bookmark's smudge, dust cover,
fantastical abstract swirl never connects,
infinitesimal, faith in its art.

It's the cracked spine that caused
all the controversy in the first place.
It detached itself during decades past.
Someone mentioned a leveler,
fallacies remain unspoken.

There is a title and author on the back
cover. I thought it proper on the front.
Was it superimposed from the front
before the front came up missing?
The dust cover survived the years.

I daydream, create the beginning's story.
A swirl sets the stage for every lost page
before the detachment. Please beg my
pardon, I must write carefully, as not
to reveal entirely the secret of swirl.

Secret Cottage

He says goodbye, kisses his child.
A ferry ferries him back across a lake.
His, a secret cottage no phone, no roads.
Access – boat, swim, float.

I wish for a secret cottage.
Mine would be a houseboat.
I would watch the moose, bear, deer, come to drink from shore.
I would gaze at ducks, geese- watch them float, fly off overhead.
My secret unravels as beast, fowl, watch my house float by them.
My heart yearns to keep secret my floating house.

I say goodbye, kiss my child on shore.
My child launches his kayak, paddles toward his home.
His, the secret cottage where no roads lead,
the one with no phone.

my poem is a parachute

wind lifts me sideways
I stretch, limbs sway,
release of parachute
ripcord gives way.

swiftly I drift
destination earthbound,
my poem is a parachute
thrill seeker, clown.

parachute's faded script
secret on the breeze,
riddled with rainbows
day-star released.

my poem is a parachute
letters graze azure sky
streak-silver into ether
claims no alibi.

lush

unfurl twirl swirl
chartreuse jade lime
shade sun rainforest
undergrowth overgrowth
fronds feathery
quake quiver
fiddlehead beech
maidenhair
sporangia rhizoids
antheridia archegonia
climb float resurrect
meadows forest
lakes streams
floral accoutrement
wispy whisperer
graceful lush angelical
my mother's middle name
my friend, the fern

My Ambrosia

White rail fence exposes swollen orbs, weighty sprigs.
Deftly my finger places berry between lips.
Sweet pulp trickles as if to lend me a swig.
Nectar stains, purple tongue, juicy, sticky,
forefinger, tongue. Relentless harvest strike me numb.
I would not cease until the setting sun.

Early Ducks

Wood ducks at Lake Bomoseen,
Vermont welcome me.
In the early hours of dawn, coffee black,
I sit shore side.
Little webbed feet paddle all day long under boat docks
and rafts. Ducks search for aquatic food
and a crumb from a human hand.
Quacking persists amongst the duck clan.
Their water-speak
gives me pause. I observe their meanderings,
watch a feather float aimlessly.

Looney?

I wanted to go, I ran out of time.
No one really runs out of time unless they're dead.
It was the loon place, you know, located within the Markus
Wildlife Center in New Hampshire. I read the brochure.

I got the loon brochure from an information booth near
Weirs Beach at Lake Winnipesaukee.
The Loon Center, as it is referred to, is a 200
acre wildlife center quite a distance from the information

booth, where I ran out of time, yet I was not dead.
Now it's still on my bucket list waiting for another
trip, another information booth, another life.
I am adamant that I will get there.

It's in Moultonborough further north of Weirs Beach,
where I am reading about the loons. The Loon Center,
explains why their eyes are red, where they go in
the winter, how deep loons dive, why their chicks

ride on their parents back, and the fact that loons
are not ducks, will still be open until Indigenous
People's Day, and I should note that I could still
drive there before then, if I am not dead, or run

out of time. This would prevent my bucket list from
overflowing with all the should haves, could haves,
would haves, that I never found time to experience.
Furthermore I need to shop at the Loon Feather Shop,

"all things loon and more." I am not dead. I have not run
out of time. I should get going. The loons are calling me.

One Daffodil

One daffodil in spring has sprung
Lonely like one golden sun
Yellow hue enhance green blades
I'll not lose sight perchance it fades

A sole blossom will not stretch
Along margin of a bay
Or dance and kiss companion flowers
Instead such loneliness marks the hours

Like me who stays the course
Of time, I, its host linger long
Glorify 'til blossom's gone
Petal refuse clings to ground

Without companion daffodil
A fertile earth is ripe to till
I turn a spade reflect on when
Daffodil blossom returns again

MacDonald Brook

In the middle of MacDonald Brook, Cheshire,
Massachusetts, a pail in one hand, a small net
in the other, balancing on a boulder, stooping
low, I stare into the stream eyeing critters.

I am a child. I net crayfish, minnows, water bugs.
I follow the riverbank westward through cow
pastures downstream. Here the water is deeper,
swifter. I scoop carp, suckers, from their lair, return them.

Stormy days when rain poured and the floods arrived
I was afraid. The foundation of the family home aligns with
the river's bank. As the water rises the boulders crash
against one another, and our house's foundation.

The force of the rain along with its proximity to the bridge
outside my window, begs you pack quick and get out before
the bridge succumbs to floods. Yet in the decade I lived here,
no deluge swept us or the bridge away. Once water flowed

within inches of the bridge. The foundation survived.
To this day the house still remains. I surmise the water
nymphs who flit and flutter above MacDonald Brook
have always seen to it that my childhood house still stands.

A Perfect View from the 38th Floor

The spirit of the place pulses.
Trails of heat vapor emanate
then disperse heavenward
skimming wind-whipped flags.

The infinite horizon glistens
against red mesa cliffs
like polished diamonds
cacti needles glint skyward.

Along the lost highway
ocotillo blossoms caress
scorched macadam, where
stubborn prairie grass intrudes.

Jig-sawed pavement, this
lonesome road smudges
through the desert until
it disappears along a dry

riverbed a hundred miles
west, where a range of foothills
swallow up everything except the
urgent cries of coyotes wailing

over and over, their piercing
reverberation bounces off canyons.
Once pups are comforted
the stark silence returns.

Fraught with eerie shadows,
moonlight caresses midnight.
It's then, I draw the drape, shut out
a perfect view from the 38th floor.

Tall Grasses and Willow
(written from the prompt, *Sprite*)

Faerie girl,
her willow tree
grows amongst tall pines
where no one can see
her flit and flutter
from branch to bark,
keeps her secret
of her whereabouts
after dark.

There is a knoll
which grows tall thick grasses
that shelters a troll boy
who wears glasses.
With these spectacles he
can see where she flies,
yet in the evening her
secret is with the skies.

Faerie girl dabbles in potions.
Troll boy builds gardens of devotion.
She always has a cup of dew
clenched in her hand.
He prefers dark ale from
faraway lands. His draught
quenches thirst and urges. Her potion,
camouflages for her evening excursions.

After several months, the two, well
they met. Amongst the tall grasses
below the willow tree they stumbled.
No worse did they trip then does
a humble bumble. Faerie girl and troll boy
talked and commiserated, they noted their
beverages had since gone fetid.

Alarmed each was desperate to drink.
Troll boy assured faerie that there
was hope if they could only think
of what their beverages tasted like.
Well, she said, "Sweet and clean", while his
tasted bubbly, a foamy dream.. Together they
pondered, chanted and squeezed every flower,
leaf, and fruit from his garden of devotion.

They taste-tested then sprinkled
faerie dust into a bottle, enhancing
the potion that was set into his hovel.
Faerie was patient, she knew their
elixir could not be drunk until the morrow.
Upon awakening they poured the liquid
into a vessel. Eager to swallow, and with
gusto and delight, was the maiden sip of
what is now known as spiked Sprite.

Drive

It is always this way whenever I drive this stretch of road.
Hawk, deer, a rafter of turkey greet me. In summer's drought
dust kicks up behind car. In fall deciduous canopy, vivid
brilliance leaves me in a stupor as airborne leaves float aimlessly.

In winter it can be traversed by snowshoes, X-country skis
snowmobiles. A poet once said, "sled dogs, Linda, sled dogs!"
I google Malamute, stare into the eyes of a canine revered
for strength and resistance to cold, taxi for the snowbound.

Spring is always dicey, dirt shoulder, sucks tire in
a phantom mud slick. The road meanders upward like
a ski slope. As I ascend, my eyes peer over the rise.
An overlook; notification that you have arrived begs

you stay and soak up a valley's contents: roads, rivers, lakes,
rooftops, chimneys, vehicles, houses, windmills, schools,
churches, cell towers, meadows, farms, fields, forests- entities;
a living testament to humans who've laid the bricks,

sawed the boards, erected the walls, roof. If it were not for the
ingenuity of those who rise to the occasion, I could not point out
my house's white roof, looming in the shadow of Mt. Greylock,
Massachusetts, a mountain donning a ninety-three foot veterans

war memorial that takes on the likeness of a lighthouse
placed in the only twelve hundred acre taiga-boreal forest
in my state. I breathe deeply, aromatic scents - pines, mountain
laurel. As I release the brake, descend, a deer stands motionless.

Easy

I roll over. Alone in bed I think of skin touching,
where it leads. I clasp my hands, feel how my
fingers make contact, I place them against my
pink cheek.

I remember how much longer your fingers were,
your hands warm and gentle in mine. We often
held hands in the car until our fingers would cramp.
You asked if we could take a break. I said,
"Letting go is not easy."

The void is real. Your ascension has taken all our easy with it.
I roll over again, notice my hands have become unclasped.

Snow Effect

A wolf's howl echoes solemnly
ominous message lost to deep caverns.
Snowflakes collapse into valleys,
light gently on eyelashes.
Each melting flake a teardrop,
her oval cheek freezes.

Winter's frigidity cannot dominate
woman cloaked in fur, a vulnerable
tenderness swept by each snowflake's
sparkle in the twilight. Coldness pains
her supple skin, so elegantly framed in mink.

Moon rising, another wolf howls.
Woman's pale lips part, her howl
pierces the frozen night. Gone!
Remnant canine prints short-lived,
drifts decimate their snow effect.

Goodnight!

Magenta leaves float on a turquoise pond,
shadows loom, wood ducks flap, fly far to shore.
Currents ripple splash over spillway. Reeds,
cattails, milkweed seeds yield, drift upon wind
currents. Jet stream seen overhead paints a
panoramic cotton road to heaven. Distant
fireball illuminates solar radiance across
mountaintop. Evening shadows slant
deep into valley's abyss. In small villages
lit windows glimmer, twilight wanes.
Holy moments of contemplation, souls
ponder meaning of life while sleepy
eyes of the world blink shut.
Goodnight!

Linda Wlodyka's, *If Brambles Were Bookend*, is a lovely exploration into the epistolary voice, at once a love letter to poetry and the lover who is the poet, and a longing for something beyond it. This something resides in the sensual details of her beautiful verse. When reading Wlodyka, one feels as if one were in a dream, in a breath of solitude and confession. I believe the kind of bramble she writes truly are bookends: they are brambles with luscious berries; they are the moments that mark our world. A delicious read.

Kika Dorsey. Colorado author of the novel, *As Joan Approaches Infinity*, by Gesture Press.

The breadth of Linda Wlodyka's poetry prowess is exemplified in the variety of subjects in *If Brambles Were Bookends*. Beat poetry, love poems, nature, ekphrastic, and even COVID all seem at home in this collection. Several of her poems address an enigmatic "you." Another writer? The reader? Or perhaps the poet herself? This is particularly striking in "Uprooted Persimmon." From her beat poem "Crushing the Eyeliner" to the sensuality of "Citrus Bomb" and the ekphrastic "Scrutiny: Sara Steele Floral" to the poignant "Easy," join Wlodyka on her mystical journey as she challenges our view of reality.

Marianne Gambaro, author of *Do NOT Stop* for Hitchhikers.

Massachusetts Beat Poetry Laureate, Linda Wlodyka adds a new bough with *If Brambles Were Bookends*. She's at her best describing heartache with rich imagery. Using her own words, this collection is a mesmerism shared by bibliophiles, a stoic shelf, an embodiment of peace waiting for the night sky, a brushstroke's caress, a couple melting together for eternity. *If Brambles Were Bookends* will leave you aching for another page to turn.

Jon Wesick. author of *The Shaman in the Library*

www.ingramcontent.com/pod-product-compliance
Lightning Source LLC
Chambersburg PA
CBHW051659090426
42736CB00013B/2443